C0-AFY-914

DATE DUE

The Library Store #47-0119

HIP-HOP

By S.L. Hamilton

VISIT US AT ABDOPUBLISHING.COM

Published by ABDO Publishing Company, 8000 West 78th Street, Suite 310, Edina, MN 55439. Copyright ©2011 by Abdo Consulting Group, Inc. International copyrights reserved in all countries. No part of this book may be reproduced in any form without written permission from the publisher. A&D Xtreme™ is a trademark and logo of ABDO Publishing Company.

Printed in the United States of America, North Mankato, Minnesota.
112010
012011

 PRINTED ON RECYCLED PAPER

Editor: John Hamilton
Graphic Design: Sue Hamilton
Cover Design: John Hamilton
Cover Photo: ThinkStock
Interior Photos: AP-pgs 14, 15, 20, 21, 24, 28 & 32; Corbis-pgs 4, 5, 26, 27 & 29; Getty Images-pgs 6, 7, 8, 9, 10, 11, 12, 13, 16, 17, 18, 19, 20 & 25; ThinkStock-pgs 1, 2, 3, 11, 21, 24 & 30.

Library of Congress Cataloging-in-Publication Data

Hamilton, Sue L., 1959-
  Hip-hop / S.L. Hamilton.
     p. cm. -- (Xtreme dance)
  ISBN 978-1-61714-731-9
  1. Hip-hop dance. I. Title.
  GV1796.H57H36 2011
  793.3--dc22

2010037639

CONTENTS

XTREME

Hip-hop mixes fast, powerful moves with rhythmic music.

HIP-HOP

Xtreme Quote

"We're looking to becoming one with that beat… To the point where your body is a musical instrument." ~Fable, b-boy

HIP-HOP

Hip-hop
became
popular in
the 1970s
in New
York City's
South Bronx.
Puerto Rican
dancers took
mambo,
cha-cha-cha,
and other
Latin dances
to the next
level.

HISTORY

Xtreme Fact

Rock Steady Crew and Dynamic Rockers were early breakdancers from New York.

DANCE

Breakdancing

Breakers use:

1) **Toprock Moves**
   (Standing up.)
2) **Downrock Moves**
   (On the floor.)
3) **Power Moves**
   (Spinning moves
   that need strength.)
4) **Freezes/Suicides**
   (Freezes hold the
   body off the ground.
   Suicides look like the
   dancer is falling or
   out of control.)

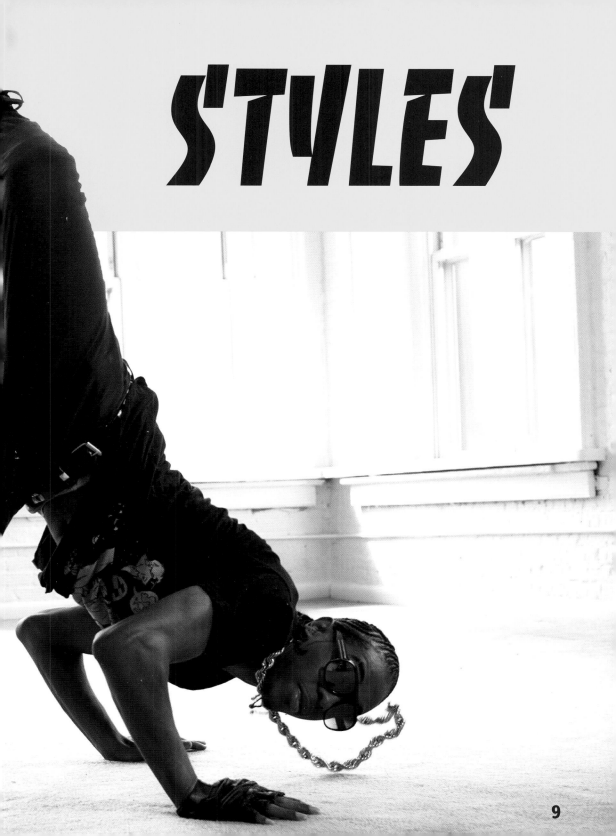

STYLES

Xtreme Quote

"I'm doing it my way."
~Don Campbell

Locking

In the late 1960s, hip-hop pioneer Don Campbell created the locking style in Los Angeles, California. While performing a dance move, he froze. He couldn't think of what to do next. Locked in place, he pointed at the audience. The pause became known as Campbellocking, or just "locking."

Popping

Popping requires a dancer's muscles to contract and release in a quick pop, jerk, or hit. Poppers use their arms, legs, chest, and neck to produce jerks to the beat of the music. The style came out of Fresno, California, in the 1970s.

"I want to show the world something they've never seen before." ~Phillip Chbeeb

Krumping

Krumping is
a freestyle,
energy-powered
dance that came
out of Los Angeles,
California, in the
1990s. Krumpers
channel anger
and hardship into
powerful, fight-like
dance moves. The
word "krump"
came from the first
letters of the phrase
"Kingdom Radically
Uplifted Mighty
Praise."

"Krumping is a high-energy mix of breakdancing, gymnastics, and spasm-like movements." ~Nicole Menzie

HIP-HOP

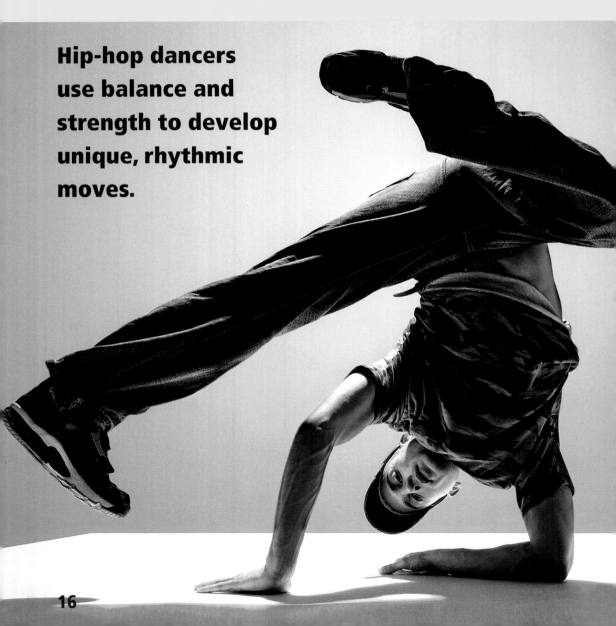

Hip-hop dancers use balance and strength to develop unique, rhythmic moves.

MOVES

X̶treme Move

A headstand is a freeze in which a dancer stands on his head with or without using hands for support.

Platform

To perform a platform, dancers place their elbows close to their sides and use their hands to hold themselves steady. Powerful muscles are needed to hold the body flat, sometimes only inches off the ground.

Xtreme Quote "Dance to express, not impress."

Hand Moves

Hip-hop dancers use their hands to hold their bodies in place. Hands also help give an ongoing flow to the dancers' moves.

Twists and Spins

Leg and body twists help dancers defy gravity, pushing them into popular hip-hop moves such as flares, swipes, spins, and windmills.

Xtreme Quote If you love it and dance from your heart, you'll find a way to do it." ~Jose Ruiz, b-boy

HIP-HOP

Tracksuits or cargo shorts with hoodies protect hip-hoppers' bodies, and are loose enough to move with the dancers.

FASHION

Female dancers are often seen in zippered jackets and jeans or jeggings. Sneakers give traction to dancers' moves. Caps and hoods protect the head.

LEARN

Beginner hip-hop moves can be learned in dance classes or by watching videos.

HIP-HOP

Top dancers learn the basics and then go on to create their own moves.

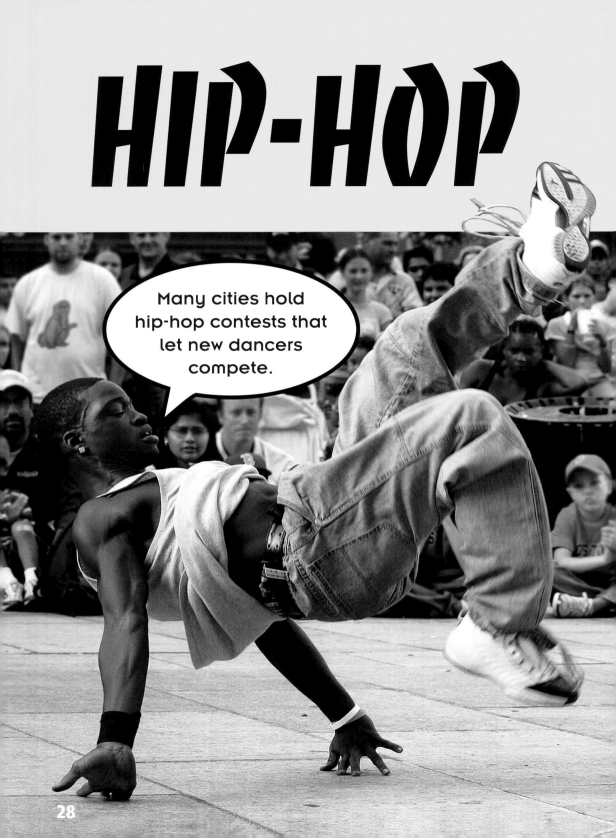

HIP-HOP

Many cities hold hip-hop contests that let new dancers compete.

BATTLES

Individual and group, or "crew," contests are called "battles." Major events include the USA and World Hip Hop Dance Championships, and Europe's Battle of the Year.

THE

B-boy / B-girl
A shortened name for male or female breakdancers.

Crew
A group of hip-hop dancers who perform together.

Flare
A move in which a dancer places his or her weight on the hands, then swings the legs in front of and behind the arms. The legs move in big circles, but only the dancer's hands touch the ground.

Freeze
A move in which a dancer remains frozen in a specific, often intense, move. A freeze is usually done at the end of a dance.

Jeggings
A style of pants often worn by b-girls. Jeggings are a mix of jeans and leggings.

GLOSSARY

Power Moves
Difficult moves that require great strength, such as head spins, flares, or windmills.

Spin
A move where a dancer spins around on his or her back, head, hands, or feet. Spins are difficult to control and require good balance.

Suicide
A move where a dancer appears to lose control and is falling, but is NOT using hands to break the fall. The move often looks very painful, but a skilled dancer knows how to fall without getting hurt.

Swipes
A power move where the top half of the body begins to spin around and the bottom half follows, creating a horizontal, circular motion.

Windmill
A move in which dancers spin from their upper back to their chest while twirling their legs in a V-shape

INDEX